S0-BXE-073

First Published in 1997 by:

EC Publishing
2391 Highland Rd.
Victoria, B.C.
V9E 1K7
(250) 474-3474
Fax (250) 474-4675

email: ercox@bc.sympatico.ca

CANADIAN CATALOGUING IN PUBLICATION DATA

Cox, Elizabeth, (Date)
Healthier Muffins

Includes Bibliographical references.
ISBN 0–9682809–0–0

1. Muffins.   2. Low-fat diet — Recipes.   I. Title.

TX770.M83C68 1997   641.8'15   C98–001603–7

Printed in Canada by Rolex Printing,
Victoria, British Columbia, Canada

Third Printing – November 1999

ABOUT THE AUTHOR

Seven years after waking up one morning with the vision of putting together a 'healthier' muffin recipe book it is finally happening.

'Heart healthy cooking' has been an everyday phrase in my family since my early teens having a father with ischemic heart disease who died at the age of 48 years. It still seems natural, even now that I have my own family, to prepare good tasting nutritious meals with lower amounts of fat and sodium.

My career in the medical field began at Prince George Regional Hospital in 1976 and in 1986 I began studying to become a Registered Cardiology Technologist passing my final exam in 1988, then going on to study for another year in the interpretation of cardiograms. I began employment at a Victoria hospital in 1988 and bringing in samples of my "heart wise" muffins for Friday coffee break treats became part of my weekly routine.

While working at the hospital on the cardiac floor, I realized the need for a recipe book containing foods that were not only lower in fat content, but which resulted in food that still tasted good so as to appeal not only to my family, but to heart patients in need of changing their eating patterns to include less fat. People are becoming more conscious of fat, cholesterol, and sodium intake as well as just counting calories and my book provides that information in an easy to follow method with a variety of delicious muffin recipes. 'Healthier Muffins' is a wonderful asset to any kitchen for the sake of our families and our hearts.

Elizabeth Cox

ACKNOWLEDGEMENTS

With love to my family and friends

***

Thank you to Mom and Dad for endless support and reassurance that dreams and ambitions are worth striving for

***

Thank you also to Dr. W. Glenn Friesen for his positive encouragement and his willingness to share his knowledge

INTRODUCTION

In today's health conscious society good food constitutes the framework of a healthy body and mind. We encourage the revival of more natural ways of food preparation than was seen during the pre-processed days. Medical doctors are changing their approach to healing in response to overwhelming evidence of the importance of food to our general health. Although there is much controversy regarding effects of diet on health, data is emerging that is leading people to a lifestyle more conscious of good eating habits and total body fitness. Studies show that consumption of some elements of our diet need to be greatly reduced.

Many people worry that good taste has to be compromised for good health but I have tried to create a collection of muffin recipes that are not only delicious, but also nutritious, low in cholesterol, low in fat, and that contain reduced amounts of sodium. Each recipe is accompanied by a listing of the total number of calories, grams of fat, milligrams of cholesterol and milligrams of sodium contained in each muffin. It must be realized that these figures are approximate, as the market is abundant with nutritional counters that vary in their calculations. When compiling these recipes I have utilized the most naturally wholesome ingredients that are readily available to today's consumer.

A word about oils. Although it is realized that we lose the benefit of a good oil when it is heated, baking is less destructive to oils than frying. The temperature in the batter reaches approximately 100 Degrees C and only the crust is actually baked. The less oils are heated, the less they are destroyed and the better they are for us.

Healthier Muffins was written not only for individuals who are on calorie, fat, cholesterol or sodium reduced eating programs, but is also for people who are in touch with the nutritional aspects of their daily diet and who still enjoy a warm tasty muffin fresh from the oven.

THE PERFECT MUFFIN

Light and tender with a rough, shiny, golden
crust. Perfect as a healthy snack or as
part of a healthy meal.

****

Muffins are a delicious and nutritious snack
that are economical and quickly made.

TURNING OUT
THE PERFECT MUFFIN:

Ingredients should be fresh and stored in the proper way so as to preserve the freshness.

> Natural bran, oatbran, wheatgerm, walnuts and whole wheat flour store well in the refrigerator or freezer compartment of the fridge. Storing at room temperature for long periods will cause wheatgerm and walnuts to turn rancid.

> Dry ingredients such as flour and dried fruits store well at room temperature in plastic containers.

> Brown sugar will not harden if stored in the fridge or freezer compartment of the refrigerator.

Muffin batter should be lumpy as over mixing causes tunnels and a tough texture. When filling muffin cups scoop enough batter on a spoon to fill cup to the required depth.

For easy removal of muffins from pan, and for easy clean up, use a spray vegetable oil to coat muffin tin before filling with batter. (NOTE: paper liners are not recommended for the recipes in this book due to the reduced amounts of oil used)

CONTENTS

COFFEE BREAK?

BREAKFAST

MUFFINS

APPLESAUCE MUFFINS

1/3 cup vegetable oil	75 mL
1/2 cup brown sugar	125 mL
(reserve 1 Tbs. (15mL))	
1/2 tsp. vanilla	2 mL
3 egg whites	3
2 tsp. baking soda	10 mL
2 cups unsweetened applesauce	500 mL
2 cups whole wheat flour	500 mL
1/4 tsp. ground cloves	1 mL
1/4 tsp. cinnamon	1 mL
1/4 cup chopped dates	50 mL
1/2 cup currants	125 mL

In small bowl combine oil, sugar (except reserved portion), vanilla and egg whites. In separate bowl dissolve baking soda in applesauce and add to liquid mixture. In large bowl stir together remaining ingredients (except reserved sugar). Pour liquid ingredients over dry mixture stirring just until moistened. Fill greased muffin cups 3/4 full. Combine reserved sugar with 1/2 tsp (2 mL) cinnamon and sprinkle on top of batter.

BAKE: 375 Degrees F
190 Degrees C

TIME: 25 - 30 Minutes

YIELD: 12 Large

PER MUFFIN:

CALORIES	202
grams FAT	6.4
mg CHOLESTEROL	none
mg SODIUM	35

"Another great way to use more of that home-made applesauce"

APPLESAUCE DATE MUFFINS

2 egg whites	2
1/2 cup unsweetened apple juice	125 mL
1/4 cup vegetable oil	50 mL
1 tsp. vanilla	5 mL
1/2 tsp. baking soda	2 ml
1 cup unsweetened applesauce	250 mL
1 1/2 cups unbleached flour	375 mL
1/2 cup rolled oats	125 mL
1/4 cup lightly packed brown sugar	50 mL
1 Tbs. baking powder	15 mL
1/4 cup finely chopped walnuts	50 mL
1/4 cup chopped dates	50 mL

In small bowl combine egg whites, apple juice, oil and vanilla mixing well. In separate bowl stir baking soda into applesauce, then stir into liquid mixture. In large mixing bowl stir together flour, oats, sugar and baking powder. Pour liquid mixture over dry ingredients stirring just until moistened. Fold in nuts and dates. Fill greased muffin cups 3/4 full.

BAKE: 375 Degrees F   **TIME:** 20 - 25 Minutes
190 Degrees C

YIELD: 12 Medium

PER MUFFIN:

CALORIES	163
grams FAT	5.8
mg CHOLESTEROL	none
mg SODIUM	34

APPLESAUCE OATMEAL MUFFINS

1 cup rolled oats	250 mL
1 cup low fat buttermilk	250 mL
1/4 cup vegetable oil	50 mL
1/3 cup brown sugar	75 mL
3 egg whites	3
1 tsp. vanilla	5 mL
1 1/2 cups unbleached flour	375 mL
1/2 cup whole wheat flour	125 mL
1/2 tsp. cinnamon or cardamom	2 mL
1 tsp. baking powder	5 mL
1/2 cup raisins or currants	125 mL
1/4 cup chopped walnuts	50 mL
1 tsp. baking soda	5 mL
1 1/2 cups unsweetened applesauce	375 mL

In small bowl combine rolled oats and buttermilk and let stand. In separate bowl blend together oil, sugar, egg whites and vanilla. In large mixing bowl stir together flours, cinnamon (or cardamom) and baking powder. Fold in currants and walnuts. Stir baking soda into applesauce then combine all liquid ingredients together. Pour over dry mixture stirring just until moistened. Fill greased muffin cups near full.

BAKE: 400 Degrees F   **TIME:** 25 - 30 Minutes
200 Degrees C

YIELD: 15 Medium

PER MUFFIN:

CALORIES	166
grams FAT	5.2
mg CHOLESTEROL	trace
mg SODIUM	55

APRICOT OATMEAL BRAN MUFFINS

1 cup boiling water	250 mL
3/4 cup natural bran	175 mL
1 1/2 cups unbleached flour	375 mL
1 cup whole wheat flour	250 mL
1/3 cup wheat germ	75 mL
2 1/2 tsp. baking soda	12 mL
1/2 cup vegetable oil	125 mL
3/4 cup brown sugar	175 mL
3 egg whites	3
2 cups low fat buttermilk	500 mL
2 cups rolled oats	500 mL
1 cup chopped apricots	250 mL

Pour boiling water over bran and let stand. In large bowl stir together flours, wheat germ and baking soda. In smaller bowl mix together oil, sugar, egg whites and buttermilk stirring well to blend. Add liquid mixture to dry ingredients stirring just until moistened. Fold in oats, apricots and bran mixture. Fill greased muffin cups 3/4 full.

BAKE: 375 Degrees F
190 Degrees C

TIME: 15 - 22 Minutes

YIELD: 24 Medium

PER MUFFIN:

CALORIES	170
grams FAT	5.3
mg CHOLESTEROL	trace
mg SODIUM	27

BANANA OAT MUFFINS

1/2 cup whole wheat flour	125 mL
1/2 cup unbleached flour	125 mL
1/2 cup rolled oats	125 mL
1 tsp. baking soda	5 mL
1 tsp. baking powder	5 mL
2 egg whites	2
1/3 cup granulated sugar	75 mL
1/4 cup vegetable oil	50 mL
1 1/2 cups mashed banana (3-4 bananas)	375 mL
1 tsp. vanilla	5 mL

In large mixing bowl combine flours, oats, baking soda and baking powder . In smaller bowl mix remaining ingredients until well blended. Pour liquid over dry ingredients stirring just until moistened. Fill greased muffin cups 2/3 full.

BAKE: 375 Degrees F   **TIME:** 20 - 25 Minutes
190 Degrees C

YIELD: 12 Medium

PER MUFFIN:

CALORIES	138
grams FAT	5
mg CHOLESTEROL	none
mg SODIUM	34

BANANA WHEATGERM MUFFINS

1 cup unbleached flour	250 mL
1/2 cup whole wheat flour	125 mL
2/3 cup wheat germ	150 mL
1/3 cup brown sugar	75 mL
1/2 tsp. baking soda	2 mL
2/3 cup skim milk yogurt	150 mL
1/4 cup vegetable oil	50 mL
2 egg whites	2
1 tsp. vanilla	5 mL
1 cup mashed banana (2 - 3 bananas)	250 mL

In large mixing bowl stir together dry ingredients. In smaller bowl blend yogurt, oil, egg whites, vanilla and mashed bananas. Pour liquid over dry ingredients stirring just until moistened. Fill greased muffin cups 3/4 full.

BAKE: 400 Degrees F   **TIME:** 20 - 25 Minutes
200 Degrees C

YIELD: 10 Medium

PER MUFFIN:

CALORIES	195
grams FAT	6.6
mg CHOLESTEROL	trace
mg SODIUM	22

BERRY BRAN MUFFINS

2 cups bran cereal (not flakes)	500 mL
1 1/2 cups skim milk	375 mL
1 cup blackberries or raspberries	250 mL
2 Tbs. granulated sugar	30 mL
1/2 cup unbleached flour	125 mL
1/2 cup whole wheat flour	125 mL
1 Tbs. baking powder	15 mL
1/4 cup honey	50 mL
2 Tbs. vegetable oil	30 mL
2 egg whites	2
1 1/2 tsp. vanilla	7 mL

In small bowl mix cereal and milk together and let stand 10 minutes stirring several times. In another bowl mix berries and sugar, set aside. In a large bowl stir together flours and baking powder. Stir honey, oil, egg whites, vanilla and berry mixture into cereal. Pour over dry ingredients stirring just until moistened. Fill greased muffin cups to the top.

BAKE: 400 Degrees F   **TIME:** 20 - 25 Minutes
200 Degrees C

YIELD: 12 Large

PER MUFFIN:

CALORIES	125
grams FAT	2.6
mg CHOLESTEROL	trace
mg SODIUM	188

BLUEBERRY CINNAMON MUFFINS

1 cup unbleached flour	250 mL
1/2 cup whole wheat flour	125 mL
1 Tbs. cinnamon	15 mL
2 tsp. baking powder	10 mL
1/2 tsp. baking soda	5 mL
1/2 cup brown sugar	125 mL
2 egg whites	2
1 cup low fat buttermilk	250 mL
1/4 cup vegetable oil	50 mL
1/2 tsp. vanilla	2 mL
1 1/2 cups blueberries	375 mL
1 Tbs. granulated sugar	15 mL

In large bowl stir together flours, half the cinnamon, baking powder and soda. Stir in brown sugar. In separate bowl combine egg whites, buttermilk, oil and vanilla. Pour liquid mixture over dry ingredients stirring just until moistened. Fold in blueberries. Fill greased muffin cups 2/3 full. Sprinkle the 1 tablespoon of granulated sugar mixed with remaining cinnamon over batter before baking.

BAKE: 375 Degrees F
190 Degrees C

TIME: 20 - 25 Minutes

YIELD: 12 Medium

PER MUFFIN:

CALORIES	152
grams FAT	4.9
mg CHOLESTEROL	trace
mg SODIUM	85

"For a seasonal touch, replace half the blueberries with halved cranberries"

BLUEBERRY OAT MUFFINS

1 cup rolled oats	250 mL
1 cup low fat buttermilk <u>or</u> sour milk*	250 mL
1/2 cup unbleached flour	125 mL
1/2 cup whole wheat flour	125 mL
1 tsp. baking powder	5 mL
1/2 tsp. baking soda	2 mL
1/2 cup brown sugar	125 mL
2 egg whites	2
1/4 cup vegetable oil	50 mL
1 cup blueberries	250 mL

* Add 1 Tbs. (15 mL) vinegar <u>or</u> lemon juice to one cup (250mL) skim milk and use as directed

In small bowl combine oats and buttermilk <u>or</u> sour milk. Let stand. In large bowl stir together flour, baking powder, baking soda and brown sugar. To oat mixture add egg whites and oil stirring well to blend. Add liquid mixture to dry ingredients stirring just until moistened. Fold in blueberries. Fill greased muffin cups 3/4 full.

BAKE: 400 Degrees F
200 Degrees C

TIME: 15 - 20 Minutes

YIELD: 12 Medium

PER MUFFIN:

CALORIES	156
grams FAT	5
mg CHOLESTEROL	trace
mg SODIUM	51

BRAN MUFFINS

1/4 cup vegetable oil	50 mL
1/4 cup molasses	50 mL
3 egg whites	3
1 cup skim milk	250 mL
1 1/2 cups natural bran	375 mL
1/2 cup unbleached flour	125 mL
1/2 cup whole wheat flour	125 mL
1 1/2 tsp. baking powder	7 mL
1/2 tsp. baking soda	2 mL
1/2 cup raisins or finely chopped dates	125 mL

In small bowl blend together oil, molasses, egg whites and skim milk. Stir in bran. In large mixing bowl stir together dry ingredients. Pour liquid mixture over dry ingredients stirring just until moistened. Fold in raisins or dates. Fill greased muffin cups 2/3 full.

BAKE: 400 Degrees F   **TIME:** 20 Minutes
200 Degrees C

YIELD: 12 Medium

PER MUFFIN:

CALORIES	132
grams FAT	5
mg CHOLESTEROL	trace
mg SODIUM	74

100 % BRAN BLUEBERRY MUFFINS

1 cup 100 % bran cereal	250 mL
1 cup rolled oats	250 mL
1 1/4 cups skim milk	300 mL
1 Tbs. vinegar	15 ml
2 egg whites	2
1/2 cup honey	125 mL
1/3 cup vegetable oil	75 mL
1 1/2 cups unbleached flour	375 mL
1 Tbs. baking powder	15 mL
1/2 tsp. cinnamon	2 mL
1 1/2 cups blueberries	375 mL

In small bowl combine cereal and rolled oats. Stir in skim milk and vinegar and let stand 5 minutes. Stir in egg whites, honey and oil. In large bowl stir together flour, baking powder and cinnamon. Pour cereal mixture over dry ingredients stirring just until moistened. Fold in blueberries. Fill greased muffin cups 3/4 full.

BAKE: 400 Degrees F   **TIME:** 20 - 25 Minutes
200 Degrees C

YIELD: 18 Medium

PER MUFFIN:

CALORIES	147
grams FAT	4.3
mg CHOLESTEROL	trace
mg SODIUM	87

BRAN & OAT MUFFINS

1/2 cup hot water	125 mL
1 cup 100 % bran flakes cereal	250 mL
1/2 cup rolled oats	125 mL
1/2 cup chopped raisins <u>or</u> dates	125 mL
1 cup buttermilk <u>or</u> low fat yogurt	250 mL
1/4 cup vegetable oil	50 mL
2 egg whites	2
3 Tbs. honey	45 mL
1/2 tsp. vanilla	2 mL
1 1/4 cups whole wheat flour	300 mL
1 tsp. baking soda	5 mL
1/2 tsp. cinnamon	2 mL

Pour hot water over cereal and oats and let stand. In food processor or blender combine buttermilk, oil, egg whites, honey, vanilla and dates <u>or</u> raisins processing until dates are chopped. Add bran mixture and continue processing until blended. In large bowl stir together dry ingredients. Pour liquid mixture over dry ingredients stirring just until moistened. Fill greased muffin cups 2/3 full.

BAKE: 400 Degrees F   **TIME:** 15 - 20 Minutes
200 Degrees C

YIELD: 12 Medium

PER MUFFIN:
CALORIES	152
grams FAT	5.1
mg CHOLESTEROL	trace
mg SODIUM	50

BUCKWHEAT OATMEAL MUFFINS

1 cup rolled oats	250 mL
1 cup low fat buttermilk	250 mL
1 cup buckwheat flour	250 mL
1/2 cup unbleached flour	125 mL
1/2 tsp. cinnamon	2 mL
1 tsp. baking powder	5 mL
1 tsp. baking soda	5 mL
1/2 cup chopped dates	125 mL
1/3 cup honey	75 mL
1/8 cup vegetable oil	25 mL
2 egg whites	2
1/2 tsp. vanilla	2 mL
1/2 cup low fat skim milk yogurt	125 mL

In small bowl combine rolled oats with buttermilk and let stand. In larger bowl stir together flours, cinnamon, baking powder, baking soda and chopped dates. To buttermilk mixture add honey, oil, egg whites, vanilla and yogurt stirring well to blend. Pour liquid over dry ingredients stirring just until moistened. Fill greased muffin cups 3/4 full.

BAKE: 375 Degrees F
190 Degrees C

TIME: 15 - 20 Minutes

YIELD: 12 Medium

PER MUFFIN:

CALORIES	118
grams FAT	2.8
mg CHOLESTEROL	trace
mg SODIUM	62

CARROT BRAN MUFFINS

3/4 cup unbleached flour	175 mL
3/4 cup whole wheat flour	175 mL
1 1/2 cups 100 % natural bran	375 mL
1 1/2 tsp. baking soda	7 mL
1 tsp. cinnamon	5 mL
1/2 tsp. nutmeg	2 mL
1/2 cup raisins or currants	125 mL
1/4 cup chopped walnuts (optional)	50 mL
1 1/2 cups skim milk	375 mL
3 egg whites	3
2 Tbs. vinegar	30 mL
1/2 cup honey	125 mL
1/4 cup vegetable oil	50 mL
1 cup grated carrot	250 mL

In large bowl stir together dry ingredients. Fold in raisins and walnuts. In smaller bowl blend milk, egg whites, vinegar, honey, oil and grated carrot. Pour over dry ingredients stirring just until moistened. Fill greased muffin cups 3/4 full.

BAKE: 400 Degrees F   **TIME:** 20 Minutes
200 Degrees C

YIELD: 16 Medium

PER MUFFIN:	(with walnuts)	(without walnuts)
CALORIES	124	112
grams FAT	5	3.8
mg CHOLESTEROL	trace	trace
mg SODIUM	22	22

HEALTHY FRUIT NUT MUFFINS

1 1/2 cups hot water	375 mL
1/4 cup molasses	50 mL
1/2 cup All Bran	125 mL
1/2 cup rolled oats	125 mL
3 Tbs. EACH granulated sugar, brown sugar and wheat germ	15 mL each
3/4 cup whole wheat flour	175 mL
1/2 cup skim milk powder	125 mL
1 tsp. baking powder	5 mL
1/2 tsp. baking soda	2 mL
1/3 cup vegetable oil	75 mL
3 egg whites	3
1 tsp. vanilla	5 mL
1/8 cup walnuts	25 mL
1/2 cup EACH chopped dates and dried apricots	125 mL each
1/4 cup sunflower seeds (optional)	50 mL
1/2 cup raisins (optional)	125 mL

In large bowl combine water and molasses. Add bran and oats and let sit 15 minutes. In separate bowl combine sugars, wheat germ, flour, skim milk powder, baking powder and baking soda. To the bran mixture blend in oil, egg whites and vanilla and pour over dry ingredients stirring just until moistened. Fold in nuts, seeds and fruits. Spoon into greased muffin cups filling 3/4 full.

BAKE: 350 Degrees F
180 Degrees C

TIME: 20 - 25 Minutes

YIELD: 18 Medium

PER MUFFIN:	(with)	(without options)
CALORIES	179	139
grams FAT	6.4	4.9
mg CHOLESTEROL	trace	trace
mg SODIUM	67	66

HEARTY APPLESAUCE CARROT BRAN MUFFINS

2 cups natural bran	500 mL
1 1/2 cups whole wheat flour	375 mL
1/2 cup wheat germ	125 mL
2 tsp. baking powder	10 mL
2 tsp. cinnamon	10 mL
1 tsp. baking soda	5 mL
4 egg whites	4
1 1/2 cups unsweetened apple juice	375 mL
(may be substituted with skim milk)	
1 cup unsweetened applesauce	250 mL
1/2 cup vegetable oil	125 mL
1/3 cup brown sugar	75 mL
1/2 tsp. vanilla	2 mL
1/4 cup light molasses	50 mL
1 cup grated carrot	250 mL
1/2 cup chopped walnuts	125 mL
1/2 cup raisins (optional)	125 mL

In large mixing bowl stir together bran, flour, wheat germ, baking powder, cinnamon and baking soda. In smaller bowl combine egg whites, apple juice, applesauce, oil, brown sugar, vanilla, molasses and grated carrot and blend thoroughly. Add liquid ingredients all at once to dry ingredients stirring just until moistened. Fold in walnuts and raisins. Fill greased muffin cups 2/3 full.

BAKE: 375 Degrees F   **TIME:** 20 - 25 Minutes
       190 Degrees C
YIELD: 24 Medium

PER MUFFIN: (with applejuice and raisins)
CALORIES	150
grams FAT	6.2
mg CHOLESTEROL	none
mg SODIUM	35

OAT'N ORANGE MUFFINS

1 cup oat bran	250 mL
1 cup low fat buttermilk	250 mL
1/2 cup raisins	125 mL
1/4 cup orange juice	50 mL
1 Tbs. grated orange peel	15 mL
2 egg whites	2
1/2 cup honey	125 mL
1/4 cup vegetable oil	50 mL
1/2 cup unbleached flour	125 mL
1 1/2 tsp. baking powder	7 mL
1/2 tsp. baking soda	2 mL

In small bowl combine oat bran, buttermilk, raisins, orange juice and orange peel and let stand 30 minutes. In separate bowl mix together egg whites, honey and oil and add to oat bran mixture stirring well to blend. In large bowl stir together flours, baking powder and baking soda. Add oat bran mixture to dry ingredients stirring just until moistened. Fill greased muffin cups 3/4 full.

BAKE: 375 Degrees F   **TIME:** 20 - 25 Minutes
190 Degrees C

YIELD: 12 Medium

PER MUFFIN:

CALORIES	143
grams FAT	4.6
mg CHOLESTEROL	trace
mg SODIUM	68

ORANGE BLUEBERRY MUFFINS

**IN FOOD PROCESSOR OR BLENDER MIX
TOGETHER UNTIL WELL CHOPPED:**

1 whole orange (with skin)		1
1/4 cup vegetable oil		50 mL
2 egg whites		2
1/2 cup skim milk		125 mL

IN LARGE BOWL STIR TOGETHER:

1 cup unbleached flour	250 mL
1/2 cup whole wheat flour	125 mL
1/2 cup granulated sugar	125 mL
2 tsp. baking powder	10 mL
1 tsp. baking soda	5 mL

Pour processed liquid mixture over dry ingredients stirring just until moistened. Fold in one cup frozen blueberries. Fill greased muffin cups 3/4 full.

BAKE: 375 Degrees F
190 Degrees C

TIME: 20 - 25 Minutes

YIELD: 12 Medium

PER MUFFIN:

CALORIES	161
grams FAT	4.7
mg CHOLESTEROL	trace
mg SODIUM	64

"Always a Big Hit"

ORANGE BRAN MUFFINS

2 cups natural bran	500 mL
1 whole orange (with skin)	1
1/4 cup molasses <u>or</u> corn syrup	50 mL
1 1/2 cups low fat buttermilk	375 mL
1/4 cup vegetable oil	50 mL
1 tsp. vanilla	5 mL
1 1/2 cups unbleached flour	375 mL
1/2 cup whole wheat flour	125 mL
1/4 cup oat bran	50 mL
2 tsp. baking soda	10 mL
1/2 cup chopped dates	125 mL
1/4 cup chopped walnuts	50 mL

In food processor or blender combine bran, orange (cut into sections), molasses <u>or</u> corn syrup, buttermilk, oil and vanilla and blend until orange is finely chopped. Let stand 10 minutes. In large bowl stir together flours, oat bran, baking soda and salt. Stir in dates and walnuts. Pour liquid mixture over dry ingredients stirring just until moistened. Fill greased muffin cups 3/4 full.

BAKE: 400 Degrees F
200 Degrees C

TIME: 20 - 25 Minutes

YIELD: 16 Medium

PER MUFFIN:

CALORIES	151
grams FAT	4.7
mg CHOLESTEROL	trace
mg SODIUM	20

ORANGE CRUNCH MUFFINS

1 1/2 cups unbleached flour	375 mL
1/2 cup whole wheat flour	125 mL
1/3 cup granulated sugar	75 mL
1 tsp. baking powder	5 mL
1/2 tsp. baking soda	2 mL
1/2 cup malted cereal nuggets	125 mL
2 egg whites	2
1 Tbs. grated orange peel	15 mL
1 cup orange juice	250 mL
1/3 cup vegetable oil	75 ml
1/2 tsp. vanilla	2 mL

In a large mixing bowl stir together flours, sugar, baking powder and baking soda. Stir in malted cereal nuggets. In a separate bowl combine egg whites, orange peel, orange juice, oil and vanilla. Add liquid all at once to dry ingredients stirring just until moistened. Fill greased muffin cups 3/4 full.

BAKE: 400 Degrees F   **TIME:** 20 - 25 Minutes
200 Degrees C

YIELD: 12 Medium

PER MUFFIN:

CALORIES	174
grams FAT	6.2
mg CHOLESTEROL	none
mg SODIUM	66

ORANGE DATE OAT BRAN MUFFINS

1 whole orange (with skin)	1
1/2 cup chopped dates	125 mL
1/2 tsp. vanilla	2 mL
1/2 cup orange juice	125 mL
1/4 cup vegetable oil	50 mL
2 egg whites	2
1/2 cup unbleached flour	125 mL
1/2 cup whole wheat flour	125 mL
3/4 cup oat bran	175 mL
1/4 cup granulated sugar	50 mL
1 tsp. baking soda	5 mL
I tsp. baking powder	5 mL
1/2 tsp. cinnamon	2 mL
1/8 cup finely chopped walnuts	25 mL

In food processor or blender combine orange (cut into sections), dates, vanilla and orange juice. Process until finely chopped. Add oil and egg whites and process until thoroughly blended. In a large bowl stir together remaining dry ingredients reserving 1/8 cup (25 mL) of chopped walnuts for topping. Add orange mixture to dry ingredients stirring just until moistened. Fill greased muffin cups 3/4 full. Sprinkle reserved nuts on batter before baking.

BAKE: 400 Degrees F
200 Degrees C

TIME: 20 - 25 Minutes

YIELD: 12 Medium

PER MUFFIN:

CALORIES	147
grams FAT	5.8
mg CHOLESTEROL	none
mg SODIUM	34

ORANGE YOGURT MUFFINS

1/4 cup vegetable oil	50 mL
2 egg whites	2
1 whole orange (with skin)	1
1 cup skim milk yogurt	250 mL
1/2 tsp. vanilla	2 mL
1 1/2 cups unbleached flour	375 mL
1/2 cup whole wheat flour	125 mL
1/3 cup granulated sugar	75 ml
2 tsp. baking powder	10 mL
1 tsp. baking soda	5 mL
1/3 cup currants	75 ml

In food processor or blender combine oil, egg whites, orange (cut into sections), yogurt and vanilla. Process until orange is well chopped. In large mixing bowl stir together flours, sugar, baking powder and baking soda. Stir in currants. Pour liquid over dry mixture stirring just until moistened. Fill greased muffin cups to the top.

BAKE: 375 Degrees F
190 Degrees C

TIME: 25 Minutes

YIELD: 12 Medium

PER MUFFIN:

CALORIES	160
grams FAT	4.8
mg CHOLESTEROL	trace
mg SODIUM	7

ORIGINAL OAT BRAN MUFFINS

1 1/2 cups oat bran	375 mL
1 cup low fat buttermilk or	
soured skim milk*	250 mL
1/3 cup vegetable oil	75 mL
2 egg whites	2
1/2 cup brown sugar	125 mL
1/2 tsp. vanilla	2 mL
1/2 cup unbleached flour	125 mL
1/2 cup whole wheat flour	125 mL
1 1/4 tsp. baking soda	6 mL
1 tsp. baking powder	5 mL
1/2 tsp. cinnamon	2 mL
1/2 cup raisins	125 mL

*Add I Tbs. (15 mL) lemon juice or vinegar to
 1 cup (250 mL) skim milk and use as directed

Mix together oat bran and buttermilk and let stand. In small bowl blend together oil, egg whites, sugar and vanilla and add to buttermilk and oatbran mixture. In large mixing bowl stir together flours, baking soda, baking powder and cinnamon. Add liquid to dry ingredients stirring just until moistened. Fold in raisins and spoon into greased muffin cups filling 3/4 full.

BAKE: 375 Degrees F   **TIME:** 15 - 20 Minutes
          190 Degrees C

YIELD: 12 Medium

PER MUFFIN:

CALORIES	179
grams FAT	6.5
mg CHOLESTEROL	trace
mg SODIUM	60

"Delicious served with a teaspoonful of your favourite jam"

PAT'S DELICIOUS 6 WEEK BRAN MUFFINS

2 cups boiling water	500 mL
2 cups All Bran cereal	500 mL
4 cups 100 % bran flakes	1000 mL
1 cup vegetable oil	250 mL
2 1/2 cups granulated sugar	625 mL
6 egg whites	6
4 cups low fat buttermilk	1 L
3 cups unbleached flour	750 mL
2 cups whole wheat flour	500 mL
1 Tbs. cinnamon	15 mL
3 Tbs. baking soda	45 mL
1 cup raisins or chopped dates (optional)	250 mL

Pour boiling water over all bran and bran flakes and let stand. In large mixing bowl combine oil, sugar and egg whites mixing well to blend. Stir in buttermilk, then All Bran mixture. In separate bowl stir together flours, cinnamon and baking soda. Pour dry ingredients over liquid mixture stirring just until moistened. Stir in raisins or dates if desired. Keep batter in the refrigerator letting it stand 24 hours before using. Batter may be stored for up to 6 weeks in the refrigerator. To bake, fill greased muffin cups 2/3 full.

BAKE: 400 Degrees F   **TIME:** 15 - 20 Minutes
200 Degrees C

YIELD: 4 Dozen Medium

PER MUFFIN: (without raisins) (with raisins)

	(without raisins)	(with raisins)	
CALORIES	150	160	
grams FAT	4.7	4.7	
mg CHOLESTEROL	trace	trace	*"Fits perfectly into*
mg SODIUM	85	86	*a 4 litre pail"*

RAISIN BRAN MUFFINS

1 1/2 cups 100 % bran flakes	375 mL
1/2 cup raisins	125 mL
1 cup skim milk	250 mL
1/8 cup molasses	25 mL
1/8 cup granulated sugar	25 mL
1/4 cup vegetable oil	50 mL
2 egg whites	2
1 cup unbleached flour	250 mL
1 Tbs. baking powder	15 mL

In food processor or blender stir together bran flakes, raisins and milk and let stand 10 minutes. Process until raisins are well chopped. Add molasses, sugar, oil and egg whites and process just until blended. In large bowl stir together flours and baking powder. Pour liquid over dry mixture stirring just until moistened. Fill greased muffin cups 2/3 full.

BAKE: 400 Degrees F   **TIME:** 20 Minutes
200 Degrees C

YIELD: 10 Medium

PER MUFFIN:

CALORIES	142
grams FAT	5.6
mg CHOLESTEROL	trace
mg SODIUM	198

ROLLED OAT MUFFINS

2 cups rolled oats	500 mL
1 1/2 cups low fat buttermilk*	375 mL
3 egg whites	3
2 Tbs. vegetable oil	30 mL
1/2 cup unbleached flour	125 mL
1/2 cup whole wheat flour	125 mL
2 Tbs. granulated sugar	30 mL
1/4 tsp. salt	1 mL
1 tsp. baking powder	5 mL
1 1/4 tsp. baking soda	6 mL

*May be substituted with soured milk
(Add 1 1/2 Tbs. (20 mL) vinegar or lemon juice
to 1 1/2 cups (375 mL) skim milk and use as
directed)

Combine rolled oats and buttermilk or sour milk and let stand overnight. To the buttermilk mixture add egg whites and vegetable oil. In a large bowl stir together dry ingredients. Pour rolled oat mixture over dry ingredients stirring just until moistened. Fill greased muffin cups 2/3 full. Sprinkle warm muffins with icing sugar.

BAKE: 400 Degrees F   **TIME:** 25 Minutes
          200 Degrees C

YIELD: 12 Medium

PER MUFFIN:

CALORIES	122
grams FAT	3
mg CHOLESTEROL	trace
mg SODIUM	141

COFFEE

BREAK?

APPLE MUFFINS

1/4 cup vegetable oil	50mL
1/2 cup brown sugar	125 mL
2 egg whites	2
1/2 tsp. vanilla	2 mL
1 1/2 cups chopped apples with peel	375 mL
(approximately 2 large apples)	
1/4 cup orange juice	50 mL
1 cup unbleached flour	250 mL
1/3 cup whole wheat flour	75 mL
1 tsp. baking powder	5 mL
1/2 tsp. baking soda	2 mL
1/2 tsp. cinnamon	2 mL
1/4 tsp. nutmeg	1 mL

TOPPING:

1/2 tsp. (2 mL) cinnamon
1 Tbs. (15 mL) granulated sugar

In large bowl blend together oil, brown sugar, egg whites, vanilla, apple and orange juice. In a separate bowl stir together flours, baking powder, baking soda, cinnamon and nutmeg. Add all at once to apple mixture stirring just until moistened. Fill greased muffin cups 3/4 full. Stir together topping ingredients and sprinkle on batter.

BAKE: 350 Degrees F   **TIME:** 25 - 30 Minutes
180 Degrees C

YIELD: 10 Medium

PER MUFFIN:

CALORIES	169
grams FAT	5.6
mg CHOLESTEROL	none
mg SODIUM	48

APPLE BRAN STREUSEL MUFFINS

2 cups unbleached flour	500 mL
1 cup natural bran	250 mL
1/2 cup brown sugar	125 mL
1 Tbs. baking powder	15 mL
1/2 tsp. baking soda	2 mL
1 tsp. cinnamon	5 mL
2 large unpeeled apples chopped	2
1 1/3 cups low fat buttermilk	325 mL
1/4 cup vegetable oil	50 mL
3 egg whites	3

STREUSEL TOPPING:

1/4 cup unbleached flour	50 mL
1 Tbs. brown sugar	15 mL
1/2 tsp. cinnamon	2 mL
1 Tbs. vegetable oil	15 mL

In small bowl combine topping ingredients and set aside. In large mixing bowl stir together flour, bran, sugar, baking powder, baking soda, and cinnamon. Stir in chopped apples. Combine buttermilk, oil and egg whites together and pour over dry ingredients stirring just until moistened. Fill greased muffin cups 3/4 full. Sprinkle each muffin with a teaspoonful of streusel topping before baking.

BAKE: 400 Degrees F   **TIME:** 25 - 30 Minutes
200 Degrees C

YIELD: 16 Large

PER MUFFIN:

CALORIES	175
grams FAT	4.6
mg CHOLESTEROL	trace
mg SODIUM	78

BANANA AND PEANUT MUFFINS

1 cup unbleached flour	250 mL
3/4 cup whole wheat flour	175 mL
1/4 cup low fat soya flour	50 mL
(may be substituted with unbleached flour)	
1/4 cup brown sugar	50 mL
2 tsp. baking powder	10 mL
1 tsp. baking soda	5 mL
1/4 tsp. nutmeg	1 mL
1/2 cup chopped unsalted peanuts	125 mL
2 egg whites	2 mL
1 3/4 - 2 cups mashed ripe bananas	425 - 500 mL
(approximately 3 - 5 bananas)	
1/2 cup low fat yogurt	125 mL
1/3 cup vegetable oil	75 mL
1 tsp. vanilla	5 mL

In large mixing bowl stir together flours, sugar, baking powder, baking soda and nutmeg. Stir in peanuts. In separate bowl blend together egg whites, bananas, yogurt, oil and vanilla. Pour over dry mixture stirring just until moistened. Fill greased muffin cups 3/4 full.

BAKE: 375 Degrees F   **TIME:** 25 Minutes
190 Degrees C

YIELD: 16 Medium

PER MUFFIN:
CALORIES	161
grams FAT	6
mg CHOLESTEROL	trace
mg SODIUM	24

BANANA GRAHAM MUFFINS

1 cup graham wafer crumbs	250 mL
(approximately 16 crackers)	
3/4 cup unbleached flour	175 mL
1/4 cup brown sugar	50 mL
1 tsp. baking powder	5 mL
1/2 tsp. cinnamon	2 mL
1 tsp. baking soda	5 mL
2 egg whites	2
1/4 cup vegetable oil	50 mL
1 cup mashed banana (2-3 bananas)	250 mL

In large bowl stir together dry ingredients. In separate bowl combine liquid ingredients and mashed banana stirring well to blend. Pour liquid over dry ingredients stirring just until moistened. Fill greased muffin cups 3/4 full.

BAKE: 375 Degrees F   **TIME:** 20 - 25 Minutes
190 Degrees C

YIELD: 10 Medium

PER MUFFIN:

CALORIES	171
grams FAT	5.5
mg CHOLESTEROL	none
mg SODIUM	97

BLUEBERRY YOGURT MUFFINS

1 1/2 cups unbleached flour	375 mL
1 cup whole wheat flour	250 mL
1/2 cup granulated sugar	125 mL
1 tsp. baking soda	5 mL
1 cup skim milk yogurt	250 mL
3 egg whites	3
1 tsp. vanilla	5 mL
1/4 cup vegetable oil	50mL
1 1/4 cups frozen blueberries	300 mL

In large bowl combine flours, sugar and baking soda. In smaller bowl blend together yogurt, egg whites, oil and vanilla. Pour liquid over dry ingredients stirring just until moistened. Fold in blueberries. Spoon batter into greased muffin cups filling 3/4 full.

BAKE: 400 Degrees F
200 Degrees C

TIME: 20 Minutes

YIELD: 12 Large

PER MUFFIN:

CALORIES	181
grams FAT	4.6
mg CHOLESTEROL	trace

CAROB OAT MUFFINS

1 cup rolled oats	250 mL
1 cup low fat buttermilk	250 mL
1/2 cup unbleached flour	125 mL
1/2 cup whole wheat flour	125 mL
1/3 cup granulated sugar	75 mL
1/3 cup carob powder	75 mL
1 tsp. baking powder	5 mL
1 tsp. baking soda	5 mL
1 tsp. cinnamon	5 mL
1/4 cup chopped walnuts	50 mL
1/3 cup carob chips	75 mL
2 egg whites	2
1/4 cup vegetable oil	50 mL
1 tsp. vanilla	5 mL

Combine oats and buttermilk and let stand. In large bowl stir together flours, sugar, carob powder, baking powder, baking soda, cinnamon, walnuts and carob chips. To oat mixture add egg whites, oil and vanilla stirring well to blend. Pour over dry ingredients stirring just until moistened. Fill greased muffin cups 2/3 full. After baking, while still warm, sprinkle with icing sugar.

BAKE: 400 Degrees F
200 Degrees C

TIME: 20 Minutes

YIELD: 12 Medium

PER MUFFIN:

CALORIES	150
grams FAT	6
mg CHOLESTEROL	trace
mg SODIUM	54

CARROT OAT MUFFINS

1 cup rolled oats	250 mL
1 cup low fat buttermilk or	
sour skim milk*	250 mL
1/2 cup unbleached flour	125 mL
1/2 cup whole wheat flour	125 mL
1/2 tsp. baking soda	2 mL
2 egg whites	2
1/2 cup brown sugar	125 mL
1/4 cup vegetable oil	50 mL
1 tsp. vanilla	5 mL
1 cup (packed) grated carrot	250 mL
1/2 cup raisins	125 mL
1 Tbs. sesame seeds	15 mL

* Add one tablespoon (15 mL) lemon juice or vinegar to one cup skim milk and use as directed.

In small bowl combine rolled oats with buttermilk and let stand. In large mixing bowl stir together flours and baking soda. To buttermilk mixture add egg whites, brown sugar, oil, vanilla and grated carrot stirring well to blend. Add liquid mixture all at once to dry ingredients stirring just until moistened. Fold in raisins. Fill greased muffin cups 3/4 full. Sprinkle batter with sesame seeds before baking.

BAKE: 400 Degrees F
200 Degrees C

TIME: 15 - 20 Minutes

YIELD: 16 Medium

PER MUFFIN:

CALORIES	172
grams FAT	5.9
mg CHOLESTEROL	trace
mg SODIUM	63

CARROT PINEAPPLE MUFFINS

1/2 cup granulated sugar	125 mL
3 egg whites	3
1/4 cup vegetable oil	50 mL
1 tsp. vanilla	5 mL
1 cup grated carrot (packed)	250 mL
1/2 cup drained crushed pineapple	125 mL
(packed in juice)	
1 cup unbleached flour	250 mL
1/2 cup whole wheat flour	125 mL
1 tsp. baking powder	5 mL
1 tsp. baking soda	5 mL
1 tsp. cinnamon	5 mL
1/8 cup chopped walnuts (optional)	25 mL

In small bowl combine sugar, egg whites, vegetable oil and vanilla stirring well to blend. Stir in pineapple and carrots. In large mixing bowl stir together flours, baking powder, baking soda and cinnamon. Stir in walnuts. Pour liquid ingredients over dry mixture stirring just until moistened. Fill greased muffin cups 3/4 full.

BAKE: 350 Degrees F   **TIME:** 25 Minutes
       180 Degrees C

YIELD: 12 Medium

PER MUFFIN:	(with walnuts)	(without walnuts)
CALORIES	172	164
grams FAT	5.5	4.8
mg CHOLESTEROL	none	none
mg SODIUM	43	40

CARROT RAISIN MUFFINS

3/4 cup whole wheat flour	175 mL
3/4 cup unbleached flour	175 mL
1 tsp. baking powder	5 mL
1 tsp. baking soda	5 mL
1 tsp. cinnamon	5 mL
1/2 tsp. ginger	2 mL
1/2 tsp. allspice	2 mL
1/2 cup brown sugar	125 mL
2 egg whites	2
1/2 cup low fat buttermilk	
or sour skim milk*	125 mL
1/4 cup vegetable oil	50 mL
1/2 tsp. vanilla	2 mL
1 1/2 cups grated carrot	375 mL
1/2 cup raisins	125 mL

*Add 1 1/2 tsp. (7mL) vinegar or lemon juice to
1/2 cup (125 mL) skim milk and use as directed

In a large bowl combine dry ingredients stirring well to blend. In smaller bowl mix together egg whites, buttermilk, oil and vanilla. Stir in carrots and raisins. Pour liquid over dry ingredients stirring just until moistened. Fill greased muffin cups 2/3 full.

BAKE: 400 Degrees F   **TIME:** 15 - 20 Minutes
200 Degrees C

YIELD: 10 Medium

PER MUFFIN:

CALORIES	166
grams FAT	5.6
mg CHOLESTEROL	trace
mg SODIUM	53

COFFEE CAKE MUFFINS

1 cup unbleached flour	250 mL
1/2 cup whole wheat flour	125 mL
1/3 cup granulated sugar	75 mL
2 tsp. baking powder	10 mL
2 egg whites	2
1/2 cup skim milk	125 mL
1/2 tsp. vanilla	2 mL
1/4 cup vegetable oil	50 mL
(Reserve 1 Tbs. (15 mL))	
FILLING:	
2 Tbs. brown sugar	30 mL
1/8 cup finely chopped walnuts	25 mL
1 Tbs. unbleached flour	15 mL
1 tsp. cinnamon	5 mL
Reserved vegetable oil	

In large bowl combine flours, sugar and baking powder. In separate bowl stir together egg whites, milk, vanilla and oil (except reserved portion). Pour liquid mixture over dry ingredients stirring just until moistened. For filling stir together filling ingredients in small bowl. Spoon half the batter into 10 greased muffin cups. Sprinkle portion of filling into each muffin cup then top with remaining batter.

BAKE: 350 Degrees F
180 Degrees C

TIME: 20 - 25 Minutes

YIELD: 10 Medium

PER MUFFIN:

CALORIES	141
grams FAT	6.5
mg CHOLESTEROL	trace
mg SODIUM	47

CORNBERRY MUFFINS

1/2 cup whole wheat flour	125 mL
1/4 cup rolled oats	50 mL
1 cup cornmeal	250 mL
1/4 cup wheat germ	50 mL
1 1/2 tsp. baking soda	7 mL
2/3 cup low fat buttermilk	150 mL
1/4 cup plus 3 Tbs. pure apple juice concentrate	95 mL
2 egg whites	2
1/4 cup vegetable oil	50 mL
1 cup fresh or frozen blueberries	250 mL

In large bowl stir together flour, rolled oats, cornmeal, wheat germ and baking soda. In separate bowl blend together buttermilk, apple juice concentrate, egg whites and oil. Pour over dry ingredients stirring just until moistened. Fold in blueberries. Fill greased muffin cups 2/3 full.

BAKE: 400 Degrees F   **TIME:** 15 - 20 Minutes
200 Degrees C

YIELD: 12 Medium

PER MUFFIN:

CALORIES	150
grams FAT	5.5
mg CHOLESTEROL	trace
mg SODIUM	23

DONNA'S ORANGE WHEATGERM MUFFINS

1 1/2 cups wheat germ	375 mL
1 1/2 cups whole wheat flour	375 mL
2 tsp. baking powder	10 mL
1 tsp. baking soda	5 mL
1/2 cup raisins	125 mL
1/4 cup vegetable oil	50 mL
2 whole oranges with skin	2
3 egg whites	3
1 cup skim milk	250 mL
3/4 cup brown sugar	175 mL

In large mixing bowl stir together wheat germ, flour, baking powder and baking soda. Stir in raisins. In food processor or blender, combine oil, oranges (cut into sections), egg whites, milk and sugar. Blend until oranges are finely chopped. Add blended mixture to dry ingredients stirring just until moistened. Fill greased muffin cups 3/4 full.

BAKE: 375 Degrees F
190 Degrees C

TIME: 15 - 20 Minutes

YIELD: 18 Medium

PER MUFFIN:

CALORIES	157
grams FAT	4.2
mg CHOLESTEROL	trace
mg SODIUM	50

DRIED APRICOT MUFFINS

1 cup chopped dried apricots	250 mL
(approximately 20 halves)	
1 cup boiling water	250 mL
(portion is reserved after draining)	
1/2 cup brown sugar	125 mL
1/4 cup vegetable oil	50 mL
1 egg white	1
1/2 tsp. vanilla	2 mL
1 cup no fat sour cream	250 mL
1 cup unbleached flour	250 mL
1 cup whole wheat flour	250 mL
1 tsp. baking soda	5 mL
1 Tbs. grated orange rind	15 mL

Soak apricots in water for 5 minutes. In large mixing bowl combine sugar, oil, egg white and vanilla. Add sour cream and mix well. Drain apricots reserving 1/4 cup (50 mL) water. Stir reserved water into liquid mixture. In separate bowl combine dry ingredients then pour over liquid mixture stirring just until moistened. Fold in apricots and orange rind. Fill greased muffin cups 3/4 full.

BAKE: 400 Degrees F   **TIME:** 18 - 20 Minutes
200 Degrees C

YIELD: 12 Medium

PER MUFFIN:

CALORIES	171
grams FAT	4.6
mg CHOLESTEROL	trace
mg SODIUM	24

GINGER MUFFINS

1/4 cup vegetable oil	50 mL
1/4 cup granulated sugar	50 mL
1/4 cup light molasses	50 mL
2 egg whites	2
1/2 tsp. vanilla	2 mL
1 cup unbleached flour	250 mL
1/2 cup whole wheat flour	125 mL
3/4 tsp. baking soda	4 mL
1/2 tsp. cinnamon	2 mL
1/2 tsp. ginger	2 mL
1/4 ground cloves	1 mL
1/2 cup hot water	125 mL

In large mixing bowl combine oil, sugar, molasses, egg whites and vanilla. In a separate bowl mix together dry ingredients and add all at once to molasses mixture. Gradually add hot water, mixing until smooth. Fill greased muffin cups 3/4 full.

BAKE: 375 Degrees F
190 Degrees C

TIME: 20 - 25 Minutes

YIELD: 9 Medium

PER MUFFIN:

CALORIES	164
grams FAT	6.1
mg CHOLESTEROL	none
mg SODIUM	20

GOLDEN GINGER MUFFINS

2/3 cup unbleached flour	150 mL
1/3 cup whole wheat flour	75 mL
2 tsp. baking powder	10 mL
1/4 tsp. ginger	1 mL
1 cup grated carrot	250 mL
1/4 cup vegetable oil	50 mL
1/4 cup brown sugar	50 mL
1 Tbs. lemon juice	15 mL
2 egg whites	2
1 Tbs. water	15 mL
1/2 tsp. vanilla	2 mL
1/4 cup raisins (optional)	50 mL

In a large mixing bowl combine flours, baking powder, and ginger. Stir in grated carrot. In a separate bowl mix together oil, brown sugar, lemon juice, egg whites, water and vanilla. Pour over dry ingredients stirring just until moistened. Fold in raisins. Fill greased muffin cups 3/4 full.

BAKE: 400 Degrees F
200 Degrees C

TIME: 20 Minutes

YIELD: 10 Small

PER MUFFIN:	(with raisins)	(without raisins)
CALORIES	128	117
grams FAT	5.5	5.5
mg CHOLESTEROL	none	none
mg SODIUM	74	74

GOLDEN SYRUP MUFFINS

1 1/2 cups whole wheat flour	375 mL
1/2 cup unbleached flour	125 mL
1/4 cup chopped walnuts	50 mL
1 1/2 tsp. baking powder	7 mL
1/2 cup currants (optional)	125 mL
2 egg whites	2
3/4 cup skim milk	175 mL
1/4 cup vegetable oil	50 mL
1/3 cup Golden Syrup	75 mL
1 tsp. vanilla	5 mL

In a large mixing bowl stir together flours, walnuts, and baking powder. Stir in currants if desired. In a separate bowl combine egg whites, milk, oil , syrup and vanilla. Add liquid mixture to dry ingredients stirring just until moistened. Fill greased muffin cups 2/3 full.

BAKE: 400 Degrees F   **TIME:** 20 Minutes
200 Degrees C

YIELD: 12 Medium

PER MUFFIN:	(without currants)	(with currants)
CALORIES	155	172
grams FAT	6.2	6.2
mg CHOLESTEROL	trace	trace
mg SODIUM	54	54

HONEY CURRANT MUFFINS

1 1/2 cups unbleached flour	375 mL
1/2 cup whole wheat flour	125 mL
1/4 cup low fat Soya flour	50 mL
(may be substituted with unbleached flour)	
1 tsp. baking powder	5 mL
1 tsp. baking soda	5 mL
1/2 cup currants	125 mL
2 egg whites	2
1/4 cup honey	50 mL
(unpasturized gives added flavor)	
1/4 cup vegetable oil	50 mL
1 cup low fat buttermilk	250 mL
1 tsp. vanilla	5 mL

In large bowl combine dry ingredients mixing well. Stir in currants. In smaller bowl blend egg whites, honey, oil, buttermilk and vanilla. Pour over dry ingredients and stir just until moistened. Fill greased muffin cups 3/4 full.

BAKE: 400 Degrees F   **TIME:** 15 - 20 Minutes
200 Degrees C

YIELD: 12 Large

PER MUFFIN:

CALORIES	166
grams FAT	5.3
mg CHOLESTEROL	none
mg SODIUM	55

"Serve warm with a teaspoonful of homemade blackcurrant jelly... delicious!"

HONEY OAT MUFFINS

1 cup rolled oats	250 mL
3/4 cup wheat germ	175 mL
1/2 cup natural bran	125 mL
1 tsp. cinnamon	5 mL
1 Tbs. orange rind	15 mL
1 cup buttermilk <u>or</u> sour skim milk*	250 mL
1/2 cup liquid honey	125 mL
3 egg whites	3
1/2 tsp. vanilla	2 mL
1/4 cup vegetable oil	50 mL
1 cup unbleached flour	250 mL
2 tsp. baking powder	10 mL
1 tsp. baking soda	5 mL
1/2 cup raisins	125 mL

* Add 1 Tbs. (15 mL) vinegar <u>or</u> lemon juice to one cup (250 mL) skim milk and use as directed

In a large bowl combine oats, wheat germ, bran, cinnamon and orange rind. Add buttermilk <u>or</u> sour milk and let stand 30 minutes. Add honey, egg whites, vanilla and oil mixing thoroughly. In separate bowl stir together flour, baking powder and baking soda and add to liquid mixture stirring just until moistened. Fold in raisins. Spoon batter into greased muffins cups filling 3/4 full.

BAKE: 375 Degrees F
190 Degrees C

TIME: 20 - 25 Minutes

YIELD: 12 Large

PER MUFFIN:

CALORIES	198
grams FAT	5.5
mg CHOLESTEROL	trace
mg SODIUM	69

LEMON BLUEBERRY MUFFINS

1 1/2 unbleached flour	375 mL
1/2 cup granulated sugar	125 mL
2 tsp. baking powder	10 mL
Rind from one lemon	
2 egg whites	2
3/4 cup skim milk	175 mL
1/4 cup vegetable oil	50 mL
1 tsp. vanilla	5 mL
1 cup fresh or frozen blueberries	250 mL

TOPPING:

1 Tbs. grated lemon rind	15 mL
1 Tbs. granulated sugar	15 mL

In large bowl stir together flour, sugar, baking powder and lemon rind. In smaller bowl blend egg whites, milk, oil and vanilla. Pour liquid over dry ingredients stirring just until moistened. Fold in blueberries. Fill greased muffin cups 3/4 full. Stir together ingredients for topping and sprinkle over batter.

BAKE: 400 Degrees F
200 Degrees C

TIME: 20 Minutes

YIELD: 12 Medium

PER MUFFIN:

CALORIES	137
grams FAT	4.7
mg CHOLESTEROL	trace
mg SODIUM	68

LEMON GINGER MUFFINS

1 cup unbleached flour	250 mL
1/2 cup whole wheat flour	125 mL
1 tsp. cinnamon	5 mL
1/3 cup rolled oats	75 mL
1/3 cup oatbran	75 mL
1/4 cup brown sugar	50 mL
1 tsp. baking soda	5 mL
1/3 cup raisins	75 mL
2 egg whites	2
1/3 cup vegetable oil	75 mL
1 cup low fat buttermilk	250 mL
1/8 cup Golden Syrup <u>or</u> molasses	25 mL
1 Tbs. grated fresh ginger	15 mL
Grated rind from one lemon	

In large mixing bowl stir together flours, cinnamon, rolled oats, oatbran, brown sugar and baking soda. Stir in raisins. In separate bowl combine egg whites, oil, buttermilk, syrup <u>or</u> molasses, ginger and lemon rind. Pour liquid over dry ingredients stirring just until moistened. Fill greased muffin cups 3/4 full.

BAKE: 400 Degrees F
200 Degrees C

TIME: 15 - 20 Minutes

YIELD: 12 Large

PER MUFFIN:

CALORIES	167
grams FAT	6.6
mg CHOLESTEROL	trace
mg SODIUM	35

"The fresh ginger is the key in this recipe"

LEMON POPPYSEED MUFFINS

2 lemons	2
1/2 cup granulated sugar	125 mL
2 cups unbleached flour	500 mL
1 cup whole wheat flour	250 mL
3 tsp. baking powder	15 mL
1 tsp. baking soda	5 mL
3 Tbs. poppyseeds	45 mL
3 egg whites	3
1 1/2 cups low fat buttermilk	375 mL
1 tsp. vanilla	5 mL
1/4 cup vegetable oil	50 mL
2 Tbs. granulated sugar	30 mL

Grate peel from lemons. Mix half the peel with the 2 Tbs. sugar and set aside. Squeeze juice from lemons. Measure out 1/2 cup of juice and stir in remaining peel. In large bowl stir together flours, 1/2 cup sugar, baking powder, baking soda and poppyseeds. In smaller bowl whisk together egg whites, buttermilk, vanilla, oil and lemon juice. Immediately add liquid mixture to dry ingredients stirring just until moistened. Fill greased muffin cups 3/4 full. Sprinkle with sugar and peel mixture before baking.

BAKE: 375 Degrees F   **TIME:** 20 - 25 Minutes
190 Degrees C

YIELD: 18 Medium

PER MUFFIN:
CALORIES	140
grams FAT	4.0
mg CHOLESTEROL	none
mg SODIUM	79

ORANGE RAISIN MUFFINS

IN SMALL SAUCEPAN SIMMER TOGETHER
5 MINUTES THEN COOL TO LUKE WARM:

1 cup pure orange juice	250 mL
1 cup raisins	250 mL

STIR INTO ORANGE JUICE MIXTURE:

1/4 cup vegetable oil	50 mL
1/3 cup liquid honey	75 mL
2 egg whites	2

IN LARGE BOWL STIR TOGETHER:

1 cup whole wheat flour	250 mL
1 cup unbleached flour	250 mL
1 tsp. baking soda	5 mL

Pour liquid mixture over dry ingredients and stir just until moistened. Fill greased muffin cups 3/4 full.

BAKE: 375 Degrees F   **TIME:** 20 - 25 Minutes
150 Degrees C

YIELD: 12 Medium

PER MUFFIN:

CALORIES	174
grams FAT	4.9
mg CHOLESTEROL	none
mg SODIUM	9

PEACHY MUFFINS

1/2 cup unbleached flour	125 mL
1/2 cup rolled oats	125 mL
1/2 cup whole wheat flour	125 mL
1/4 cup low fat soya flour	50 mL
(unbleached flour may be substituted)	
2 tsp. baking powder	10 mL
1/4 tsp. mace	1 mL
1/4 cup granulated sugar	50 mL
1/2 tsp. baking soda	2 mL
2 egg whites	2
1/2 cup low fat buttermilk	125 mL
1/2 tsp. vanilla	2 mL
1/4 cup vegetable oil	50 mL
*1 cup drained mashed peaches	250 mL
(one 398 mL can packed in pear juice)	

*VARIATION: 1 cup rhubarb sauce may be
substituted for peaches

In large bowl stir together dry ingredients. In small bowl combine remaining ingredients stirring well to blend. Pour liquid ingredients over dry ingredients stirring just until moistened. Fill greased muffin cups 3/4 full.

BAKE: 400 Degrees F   **TIME:** 20 Minutes
        200 Degrees C

YIELD: 12 Medium

PER MUFFIN:

CALORIES	126
grams FAT	5
mg CHOLESTEROL	trace
mg SODIUM	70

'PEAR'ADISE MUFFINS

1 cup unbleached flour	250 mL
1 cup whole wheat flour	250 mL
1 1/2 tsp. baking soda	7 mL
1 1/2 tsp. baking powder	7 mL
1/2 tsp. cinnamon	2 mL
1/4 tsp. nutmeg	1 mL
1 cup skim milk yogurt	250 mL
1/4 cup vegetable oil	50 mL
1/3 cup honey	75 mL
2 egg whites	2
1 Tbs. grated orange or lemon rind	15 mL
1 cup diced pears with skin on	250 mL
(canned pears packed in juice may be used)	

In large bowl stir together flours, baking soda, baking powder, cinnamon and nutmeg. In smaller bowl combine yogurt, oil, honey, egg whites, grated orange or lemon rind and diced pears. Pour over dry ingredients stirring just until moistened. Fill greased muffin cups 3/4 full.

BAKE: 400 Degrees F
200 Degrees C

TIME: 15 - 20 Minutes

YIELD: 12 Large

PER MUFFIN:

CALORIES	145
grams FAT	4.9
mg CHOLESTEROL	trace
mg SODIUM	63

PINEAPPLE MUFFINS

1 cup unbleached flour	250 mL
2/3 cup whole wheat flour	150 mL
1/3 cup low fat soya flour	75 mL
(may substitute unbleached flour)	
1/2 tsp. cinnamon	2 mL
1 tsp. baking powder	5 mL
1/2 tsp. baking soda	2 mL
1/3 cup granulated sugar	75 mL
1/4 cup vegetable oil	50 mL
1 19oz. can crushed pineapple or tidbits	
chopped fine (packed in own juice)	540 mL
2 egg whites	2
1 tsp. vanilla	5 mL

Combine dry ingredients in large mixing bowl. In small bowl stir together remaining ingredients. Pour liquid mixture over dry ingredients stirring just until moistened. Fill greased muffin cups 3/4 full.

BAKE: 400 Degrees F   **TIME:** 25 - 30 Minutes
200 Degrees C

YIELD: 12 Medium

PER MUFFIN:

CALORIES	142
grams FAT	4.9
mg CHOLESTEROL	none
mg SODIUM	82

SPICY APPLE WHEATGERM MUFFINS

1 1/2 cups unbleached flour	375 mL
1/3 cup brown sugar	75 mL
3 tsp. baking powder	15 mL
1 tsp. cinnamon	5 mL
1/4 tsp. nutmeg	1 mL
1/2 cup wheat germ	125 mL
1 cup pared, finely chopped apple (approximately 2 medium apples)	250 mL
1/2 cup currants or raisins	125 mL
1/2 cup skim milk	125 mL
1/2 tsp. vanilla	2 mL
3 egg whites	3
1/4 cup vegetable oil	50 mL

In large bowl combine flour, sugar, baking powder, cinnamon and nutmeg. Stir in wheat germ, chopped apple and raisins or currants. In separate bowl combine milk, vanilla, egg whites and oil. Add liquid ingredients all at once to dry ingredients and stir just until moistened. Fill greased muffin cups 3/4 full.

BAKE: 400 Degrees F
200 Degrees C

TIME: 20 Minutes

YIELD: 12 Medium

PER MUFFIN:

CALORIES	163
grams FAT	5.2
mg CHOLESTEROL	trace
mg SODIUM	98

SPICY FRUIT MUFFINS

1 1/2 cups unbleached flour	375 mL
1/2 cup whole wheat flour	125 mL
3 tsp. baking powder	15 mL
1/2 tsp. baking soda	2 mL
1/2 cup brown sugar	125 mL
1/2 tsp. cinnamon	2 mL
1/4 tsp. nutmeg	1 mL
1 cup shredded pared apple	250 mL
(approximately 2 medium apples)	
1/4 cup chopped walnuts	50 mL
2 egg whites	2
3/4 cup low fat buttermilk	175 mL
1/4 cup vegetable oil	50 mL
1 cup !00 % bran flakes	250 mL

In large mixing bowl combine flours, baking powder, baking soda, sugar, cinnamon and nutmeg. Stir in apple and walnuts. In separate bowl stir together egg whites, buttermilk and oil and add all at once to dry ingredients stirring just until moistened. Fold in cereal flakes. Fill greased muffin cups 2/3 full.

BAKE: 400 Degrees F   **TIME:** 15 - 20 Minutes
                200 Degrees C

YIELD: 12 Medium

PER MUFFIN:

CALORIES	187
grams FAT	6.4
mg CHOLESTEROL	trace
mg SODIUM	118

VERY RIPE BANANA MUFFINS

1/4 cup vegetable oil	50 mL
1/3 cup granulated sugar	75 mL
2 egg whites	2
1 tsp. vanilla	5 mL
1 cup (approximately) mashed bananas (2 or 3 bananas)	250 mL
1 tsp. baking powder	5 mL
1 cup unbleached flour	250 mL
1/2 cup whole wheat flour	125 mL
1 tsp. baking soda	5 mL
1/4 cup chopped walnuts (optional)	50 mL

In small mixing bowl combine oil, sugar, egg whites and vanilla. In separate bowl stir together mashed bananas and baking powder. In large bowl stir together flours, baking soda and walnuts. Blend together banana mixture with oil mixture and pour over dry ingredients stirring just until moistened. Fill greased muffin cups 1/2 full.

BAKE: 350 Degrees F
180 Degrees C

TIME: 15 - 20 Minutes

YIELD: 12 Medium

PER MUFFIN:	(with walnuts)	(without)	
CALORIES	148	132	*"Whole ripe bananas*
grams FAT	6.3	4.7	*with the skin on can*
mg CHOLESTEROL	none	none	*go directly into the*
mg SODIUM	26	23	*freezer and can be*
			taken out as needed"

ZUCCHINI MUFFINS

1 1/2 cups unbleached flour	375 mL
1/2 cup whole wheat flour	125 mL
3 tsp. baking powder	15 mL
1/2 cup granulated sugar	125 mL
1/2 tsp. cinnamon	2 mL
1/2 tsp. allspice	2 mL
1 Tbs. brown sugar	15 mL
2 cups grated zucchini	500 mL
3/4 cup skim milk	175 mL
2 egg whites	2
1/4 cup vegetable oil	50 mL

In large bowl combine flours, baking powder, sugar and spices. Add brown sugar and zucchini and toss with fork to blend. In separate bowl stir together milk, egg whites and oil and add all at once to flour mixture stirring just until moistened. Spoon into greased muffin cups filling 3/4 full.

BAKE: 400 Degrees F
200 Degrees C

TIME: 20 - 25 Minutes

YIELD: 12 Medium

PER MUFFIN:

CALORIES	151	
grams FAT	4.7	
mg CHOLESTEROL	trace	*"Grate zucchini and freeze in*
mg SODIUM	93	*two cup portions"*

LUNCHEON
&
DINNER
MUFFINS

CHEESE TOPPED CORNMEAL MUFFINS

1 cup stone-ground cornmeal	250 mL
1 cup unbleached flour	250 mL
1 tsp. baking powder	5 mL
1/2 tsp. baking soda	2 mL
1/4 tsp. salt	1 mL
2 egg whites	2
3 Tbs. vegetable oil	45 mL
2 Tbs. liquid honey	30 mL
1 1/4 cup low fat buttermilk	300 mL
4 Tbs. grated Parmesan cheese	60 mL

In large bowl combine cornmeal, flour, baking powder, soda and salt mixing well. In smaller bowl mix together egg whites, oil and honey then stir in buttermilk. Pour liquid over dry ingredients stirring just until moistened. Fill greased muffin cups 3/4 full and sprinkle each with 1 tsp. (5 mL) Parmesan cheese.

BAKE: 400 Degrees F   **TIME:** 18 - 20 Minutes
200 Degrees C

YIELD: 12 Medium

PER MUFFIN:

CALORIES	139
grams FAT	4.3
mg CHOLESTEROL	16
mg SODIUM	146

COTTAGE CHEESE MUFFINS

1/3 cup vegetable oil	75 mL
1/2 cup brown sugar	125 mL
grated rind of one lemon	1
2 egg whites	2
1 tsp. vanilla	5 mL
2 cups low fat cottage cheese	500 mL
1 1/4 cups unbleached flour	300 mL
3/4 cup whole wheat flour	175 mL
1/2 tsp. baking soda	2 mL
1 tsp. baking powder	5 mL
1/8 tsp. cardamom	.5 mL
1/2 cup raisins	125 mL

In small bowl combine oil, brown sugar, grated lemon rind, egg whites and vanilla. Stir in cottage cheese mixing until well blended. In a large bowl stir together dry ingredients and raisins. Pour liquid mixture over dry ingredients stirring just until moistened. Fill greased muffin cups 3/4 full.

BAKE: 350 Degrees F
180 Degrees C

TIME: 30 Minutes

YIELD: 12 Large

PER MUFFIN:

CALORIES	209
grams FAT	6.4
mg CHOLESTEROL	trace
mg SODIUM	187

DILLED CHEESE MUFFINS

1 cup unbleached flour	250 mL
1/3 cup whole wheat flour	75 mL
1 Tbs. baking powder	15 mL
1/4 tsp. salt	1 mL
1 Tbs. granulated sugar	15 mL
1 1/2 cups grated part-skim mozzarella cheese (approximately 4 ounces)	375 mL
1/2 - 1 tsp. dried dill weed	2 - 5 mL
2 egg whites	2
2 Tbs. vegetable oil	30 mL
3/4 cup skim milk	175 mL

In large mixing bowl combine flours, baking powder, salt and sugar. Stir in grated cheese and dill weed. In smaller bowl combine egg whites, oil and milk. Add liquid mixture to dry ingredients stirring just until moistened. Fill greased muffin cups 3/4 full.

BAKE: 400 Degrees F
200 Degrees C

TIME: 20 - 25 Minutes

YIELD: 12 Medium

PER MUFFIN:

CALORIES	113
grams FAT	3.7
mg CHOLESTEROL	1.5
mg SODIUM	136

"Great served warm for lunch with caesar or fruit salad"

HERB MUFFINS

1 cup cooked brown rice, cooled	250 mL
3 Tbs. vegetable oil	45 mL
3 egg whites	3
1 cup skim milk	250 mL
1/2 tsp. vanilla	2 mL
1/4 cup grated parmesan cheese	50 mL
1/4 tsp. dried oregano	1 mL
1/4 tsp. dried basil	1 mL
1/4 tsp. marjoram	1 mL
1 1/2 cups unbleached flour	375 mL
1/2 cup whole wheat flour	125 mL
3 tsp. baking powder	15 mL

In small bowl combine cooked rice, oil, egg whites, skim milk, vanilla, cheese and herbs. In large bowl stir together flours and baking powder. Pour liquid mixture over dry ingredients stirring just until moistened. Fill greased muffin cups 3/4 full.

BAKE: 425 Degrees F
210 Degrees C

TIME: 15 Minutes

YIELD: 12 Medium

PER MUFFIN:

CALORIES	125
grams FAT	6.5
mg CHOLESTEROL	trace
mg SODIUM	93

"Great served warm with lasagna and a fresh salad"

SUNDRIED TOMATO & JALAPENO PEPPER MUFFINS

1 1/4 cups low fat buttermilk	300 mL
2 egg whites	2
1/2 small Jalapeno pepper chopped fine	
1/4 cup chopped sun dried tomatoes	50 mL
1/2 - 1 tsp. dried crushed chilies	2-5 mL
3 Tbs. vegetable oil	45 mL
2 cups unbleached flour	500 mL
2 Tbs. granulated sugar	30 mL
1 tsp. baking powder	5 mL
1 tsp. baking soda	5 mL
1/4 cup shredded Parmesan cheese	50 mL

In small bowl combine buttermilk, egg whites, pepper, tomatoes, crushed chilies and vegetable oil. In large bowl stir together flour, sugar, baking powder and baking soda. Pour liquid over dry ingredients stirring just until moistened. Fill greased muffin cups 2/3 full. Sprinkle batter with Parmesan cheese before baking.

BAKE: 400 Degrees F
200 Degrees C

TIME: 15 - 20 Minutes

YIELD: 12 Medium

PER MUFFIN:

CALORIES	133
grams FAT	4.1
mg CHOLESTEROL	trace
mg SODIUM	105

"One of my favourite meal time muffins"

TWICE CORN MUFFINS

1 1/3 cups unbleached flour	325 mL
1 Tbs. baking powder	15 mL
1/2 tsp. salt	2 mL
2 Tbs. granulated sugar	30 mL
3/4 cup cornmeal	175 mL
1/4 tsp. rosemary (optional)	1 mL
2 egg whites	2
1 cup skim milk	250 mL
1/2 tsp. vanilla	2 mL
1/4 cup vegetable oil	50 mL
1 cup frozen niblets corn thawed	250 mL

In large bowl stir together flour, baking powder, salt, sugar, cornmeal and rosemary. Stir corn into dry ingredients. In small bowl blend together egg whites, milk, vanilla and oil. Pour liquid mixture over dry ingredients stirring just until moistened. Fill greased muffin cups 3/4 full.

BAKE: 400 Degrees F   **TIME:** 25 Minutes
200 Degrees C

YIELD: 10 Medium

PER MUFFIN:

CALORIES	179
grams FAT	6
mg CHOLESTEROL	trace
mg SODIUM	233

"Excellent served with a bowl of home-made chili"

AFTER
SCHOOL

SNACKS

ANTHONY'S FAVORITE BANANA CAROB MUFFINS

1/4 cup granulated sugar	50 mL
1/4 cup vegetable oil	50 mL
1 cup mashed bananas (2 or 3 medium)	250 mL
2 egg whites	2
1 tsp. vanilla	5 mL
1/2 cup All Bran cereal	125 mL
1 cup unbleached flour	250 mL
1/2 cup whole wheat flour	125 mL
1 tsp. baking powder	5 mL
1 tsp. baking soda	5 mL
1/2 cup carob chips	125 mL

In small bowl mix together sugar, oil, banana, egg whites, vanilla and All Bran and let stand 5 minutes. In separate bowl stir together flours, baking powder and baking soda. Add liquid mixture to dry ingredients stirring just until moistened. Fold in carob chips. Fill greased muffin cups 2/3 full.

BAKE: 375 Degrees F   **TIME:** 20 - 25 Minutes
        190 Degrees C

YIELD: 12 Small

PER MUFFIN:

CALORIES	167
grams FAT	4.8
mg CHOLESTEROL	none
mg SODIUM	50

CASSIDY'S FAVORITE CAROB CHIP MUFFINS

1 1/2 cups unbleached flour	375 mL
1/2 cups whole wheat flour	125 mL
1/3 cup granulated sugar	75 mL
1/3 cup carob powder	75 mL
1 tsp. baking powder	5 mL
1/2 tsp. baking soda	2 mL
1 tsp. cinnamon	5 mL
2 egg whites	2
1 cup low fat buttermilk	250 mL
1/4 cup vegetable oil	50 mL
1 tsp. vanilla	5 mL
1/2 cup carob chips	125 mL

In large mixing bowl combine flours, sugar, carob powder, baking soda, and cinnamon. In smaller bowl mix together egg whites, buttermilk, oil, and vanilla. Pour liquid over dry ingredients and stir just until moistened. Fold in carob chips. Fill greased muffin cups 3/4 full. While still warm sprinkle baked muffins with a dusting of icing sugar.

BAKE: 400 Degrees F
200 Degrees C

TIME: 20 Minutes

YIELD: 12 Medium

PER MUFFIN:

CALORIES	155
grams FAT	5.0
mg CHOLESTEROL	trace
mg SODIUM	54

"If you don't tell them it's not chocolate, they'll never know!"

CORNMEAL JAM-BUSTER MUFFINS

1 1/2 cups cornmeal	375 mL
1 1/2 cups sour skim milk <u>or</u> low fat buttermilk *	375 mL
2 1/4 cups unbleached flour	550 mL
1/2 cup granulated sugar	125 mL
1 1/2 tsp. baking powder	7 mL
3/4 tsp. baking soda	3 mL
1/2 tsp. salt	1 mL
4 egg whites	4
1/2 cup vegetable oil	125 mL
1 tsp. vanilla	5 mL
Your favorite jam	

* Add 1 1/2 Tbs. (20 mL) vinegar <u>or</u> lemon juice to 1 1/2 cups (375 mL) skim milk and use as directed.

Combine cornmeal and sour milk <u>or</u> buttermilk and let stand for 10 minutes. In large bowl combine flour, sugar, baking powder, baking soda and salt. To cornmeal mixture add egg whites, vanilla and oil and stir until well blended. Pour over dry ingredients stirring just until moistened. Spoon batter into greased muffin cups filling to the top. With a small spoon make indentation in each muffin and fill with 1/2 tsp. (2 mL) of jam.

BAKE: 400 Degrees F
200 Degrees C

TIME: 20 - 25 Minutes

YIELD: 18 Medium

PER MUFFIN:

CALORIES	184
grams FAT	6.5
mg CHOLESTEROL	trace
mg SODIUM	89

JAM MUFFINS

2 cups unbleached flour	500 mL
1/3 cup granulated sugar	75 mL
2 tsp. baking powder	10 mL
1/4 tsp. salt	1 mL
2 egg whites	2
1 cup low fat buttermilk	250 mL
1/4 cup vegetable oil	50 mL
1 tsp. vanilla	5 mL

In large mixing bowl stir together dry ingredients. In smaller bowl mix remaining ingredients and pour over dry ingredients stirring just until moistened. Spoon batter into greased muffin cups. Place 1/2 to 1 teaspoon of your favorite homemade jam on top of each muffin and press lightly into batter with back of spoon.

BAKE: 400 Degrees F
200 Degrees C

TIME: 20 - 25 Minutes

YIELD: 12 Medium

PER MUFFIN:

CALORIES	139
grams FAT	4.9
mg CHOLESTEROL	trace
mg SODIUM	136

NATHAN'S BANANA PINEAPPLE OAT BRAN MUFFINS

2 egg whites	2
1/2 cup skim milk	125 mL
1/4 cup vegetable oil	50 mL
1/3 cup granulated sugar	75 mL
3/4 cup mashed ripe bananas	175 mL
(approximately 2 medium)	
1/2 cup chopped or crushed pineapple	125 mL
(packed in juice)	
1 tsp. vanilla	5 mL
1 cup unbleached flour	250 mL
1/2 cup whole wheat flour	125 mL
1 tsp. baking powder	5 mL
1 tsp. baking soda	5 mL
1 cup oat bran	250 mL
1/2 cup raisins	125 mL

In small bowl combine egg whites, milk, oil, sugar, banana, pineapple and vanilla and mix well. In large bowl stir together flours, baking powder, baking soda, oat bran and raisins. Pour liquid mixture over dry ingredients and stir just until moistened. Spoon into greased muffin cups filling 3/4 full.

BAKE: 400 Degrees F **TIME:** 20 - 25 Minutes
200 Degrees C

YIELD: 12 Large

PER MUFFIN:

CALORIES	184
grams FAT	5.6
mg CHOLESTEROL	trace
mg SODIUM	40

PINEAPPLE BANANA MUFFINS

2 cups unbleached flour	500 mL
1 cup whole wheat flour	250 mL
1/2 cup granulated sugar	125 mL
2 1/2 tsp. baking soda	12 mL
1 tsp. cinnamon	5 mL
4 egg whites	4
1/4 cup vegetable oil	50 mL
2 cups mashed ripe bananas	500 mL
(approximately 5 bananas)	
1 1/2 tsp. vanilla	7 mL
1 1/4 cups crushed pineapple packed in	
juice (undrained)	300 mL

In large bowl stir together flours, sugar, baking soda and cinnamon. In smaller bowl blend together oil, vanilla, egg whites, pineapple and bananas. Pour liquid over dry ingredients stirring just until moistened. Fill greased muffin cups 3/4 full.

BAKE: 350 Degrees F   **TIME:** 20 - 25 Minutes
180 Degrees C

YIELD: 18 Large

PER MUFFIN:

CALORIES	151
grams FAT	4.3
mg CHOLESTEROL	none
mg SODIUM	12

SURPRISE MUFFINS

1 3/4 cups unbleached flour	425 mL
1/3 cup granulated sugar	75 mL
1 Tbs. baking powder	15 mL
1 tsp. grated lemon rind	5 mL
3 egg whites	3
2/3 cups skim milk	150 mL
1 tsp. vanilla	5 mL
1/4 cup vegetable oil	50 mL
Your favorite jam for filling	

In large mixing bowl combine flour, sugar, baking powder and lemon rind. Stir well to blend. In smaller bowl combine egg whites, milk, vanilla and oil and add to flour mixture stirring just until moistened. Fill bottom of 12 greased muffins cups with half the batter. Form indentation in batter and fill with 1/2 tsp. (2 mL) jam. Cover with remaining batter.

BAKE: 400 Degrees F
200 Degrees C

TIME: 15 - 20 Minutes

YIELD: 12 Medium

PER MUFFIN:

CALORIES	130
grams FAT	4.7
mg CHOLESTEROL	trace
mg SODIUM	101

TAYLOR'S NO EGG BANANA MUFFINS

IN LARGE MIXING BOWL COMBINE:

1 1/2 cups unbleached flour	375 mL
1/2 cup whole wheat flour	125 mL
1 tsp. baking soda	5 mL

IN SMALL BOWL COMBINE:

1/2 cup brown sugar	125 mL
2 Tbs. vegetable oil	30 mL
1 tsp. vanilla	5 mL

IN SEPARATE BOWL STIR TOGETHER
UNTIL FOAMY:

2 Tbs. vegetable oil	30 mL
4 Tbs. water	60 mL
1 1/2 tsp. baking powder	7 mL
2 bananas mashed	2

Mix liquids together and add 2 mashed ripe bananas. Add to flour mixture and mix just until blended. Fill greased muffin cups 2/3 full.

BAKE: 400 Degrees F   **TIME:** 15 - 20 Minutes
200 Degrees C

YIELD: 12 Medium

PER MUFFIN:

CALORIES	158
grams FAT	4.8
mg CHOLESTEROL	none
mg SODIUM	53

SPECIAL
OCCASIONS

&

TRADITIONS

CRANBERRY MUFFINS

1 1/2 cups unbleached flour	375 mL
1/2 cup whole wheat flour	125 mL
1/3 cup brown sugar	75 mL
1 tsp. baking powder	5 mL
1/2 tsp. baking soda	2 mL
1/2 tsp. cinnamon	2 mL
1 cup cranberry sauce (whole berry)	250 mL
1/2 cup orange juice	125 mL
1/4 cup vegetable oil	50 mL
2 egg whites	2

In large bowl stir together dry ingredients. In small bowl combine cranberry sauce, orange juice, oil and egg whites. Pour liquid mixture over dry ingredients stirring just until moistened. Fill greased muffin cups 3/4 full.

BAKE: 400 Degrees F
200 Degrees C

TIME: 20 Minutes

YIELD: 10 Medium

PER MUFFIN:

CALORIES	200
grams FAT	5.7
mg CHOLESTEROL	none
mg SODIUM	51

"Great for using up leftover cranberry sauce during the festive season"

CRANBERRY ORANGE MUFFINS

2 egg whites	2
1/4 cup vegetable oil	50 mL
1/3 cup granulated sugar	75 mL
1 cup chopped cranberries	250 mL
(fresh or frozen)	
Grated rind of 1 large orange	
Juice of orange plus water to make	
3/4 cup liquid	175 mL
1 tsp. vanilla	5 mL
1 1/2 cup unbleached flour	375 mL
1/2 cup whole wheat flour	125 mL
2 tsp. baking powder	10 mL
1/2 tsp. baking soda	2 mL

In large bowl combine egg whites, oil and sugar . Add cranberries, orange rind, juice and vanilla mixing well to blend. In separate bowl stir together flours, baking powder and baking soda. Add to liquid ingredients stirring just until moistened. Fill greased muffin cups 3/4 full.

BAKE: 400 Degrees F   **TIME:** 15 to 20 Minutes
200 Degrees C

YIELD: 12 Medium

PER MUFFIN:

CALORIES	138
grams FAT	4.7
mg CHOLESTEROL	none
mg SODIUM	58

PUMPKIN CRUNCH MUFFINS

1 3/4 cups unbleached flour	425 mL
1/4 cup granulated sugar	50 mL
3 tsp. baking powder	15 mL
1/2 tsp. cinnamon	2 mL
1/4 tsp. ground cloves	1 mL
1/4 tsp. nutmeg	1 mL
1/2 cup raisins	125 mL
2/3 cups skim milk	150 mL
1/2 cup pumpkin (preferably fresh)	125 mL
1/4 cup vegetable oil	50 mL
2 egg whites	2
1/2 tsp. vanilla	2 mL
1 Tbs. brown sugar	15 mL

In a large bowl stir together flour, sugar, baking powder, cinnamon, cloves and nutmeg. Stir in raisins. In food processor or blender combine milk, pumpkin, oil, egg whites and vanilla. Pour over dry ingredients stirring just until moistened. Fill greased muffin cups 3/4 full. Sprinkle with brown sugar before baking.

BAKE: 400 Degrees F   **TIME:** 20 Minutes
200 Degrees C

YIELD: 12 Muffins

PER MUFFIN:

CALORIES	148	
grams FAT	4.7	
mg CHOLESTEROL	trace	*"Start a Halloween*
mg SODIUM	92	*breakfast tradition"*

SPICY HOLIDAY MUFFINS

2/3 cup skim milk	150 mL
1/2 cup pumpkin (preferably fresh)	125 mL
3 egg whites	3
1/4 cup vegetable oil	50 mL
1 tsp. vanilla	5 mL
1 1/4 cup unbleached flour	300 mL
1/2 cup whole wheat flour	125 mL
1/4 cup granulated sugar	50 mL
3 tsp. baking powder	15 mL
1/4 tsp. cardamom	1 mL
1/2 tsp. cinnamon	2 mL
1/4 tsp. nutmeg	1 mL
TOPPING:	
1/4 cup finely chopped walnuts	50 mL
2 Tbs. granulated sugar	30 mL
1/4 tsp. cinnamon	1 mL

In small bowl combine milk, pureed pumpkin, egg whites, oil and vanilla. In large bowl stir together dry ingredients. Pour liquid mixture over dry ingredients stirring just until moistened. Fill greased muffin cups 3/4 full. Mix topping ingredients together and sprinkle batter with mixture.

BAKE: 400 Degrees F   **TIME:** 20 - 25 Minutes
200 Degrees C

YIELD: 15 Medium

PER MUFFIN:

CALORIES	121
grams FAT	5
mg CHOLESTEROL	trace
mg SODIUM	76

SPICY PUMPKIN MUFFINS

1 cup unbleached flour	250 ml
1/2 cup whole wheat flour	125 mL
1/4 cup soya <u>or</u> unbleached flour	50 mL
1/4 cup brown sugar	50 mL
3 tsp. baking powder	15 mL
1/2 tsp. cinnamon	2 mL
1/4 tsp. allspice	1 mL
1/4 tsp. mace	1 mL
1/4 tsp. ground cloves	1 mL
1/2 cup currants	125 mL
2/3 cup skim milk	150 mL
1/2 cup pumpkin (preferably fresh)	125 mL
1/4 cup vegetable oil	50 mL
2 egg whites	2
1 tsp. vanilla	5 mL
TOPPING: 2 Tbs. brown sugar	30mL

In large bowl combine flours, sugar (excluding topping), baking powder, cinnamon, allspice, mace and cloves. Stir in currants. In food processor or blender combine milk, pumpkin, oil, egg whites and vanilla. Process until well blended. Pour over dry ingredients stirring just until moistened. Fill greased muffin cups 3/4 full. Sprinkle a small portion of brown sugar over batter before baking.

BAKE: 400 Degrees F   **TIME:** 20 Minutes
200 Degrees C
YIELD: 12 Medium

PER MUFFIN:

CALORIES	148
grams FAT	5.0
mg CHOLESTEROL	trace
mg SODIUM	91

NOTES

NOTES

NOTES

NOTES

BIBLIOGRAPHY

Count Your Calories. New York. Dell Publishing Company, 1978

Erasmus, Udo _Fats and Oils._ Vancouver. Alive Book, 1986

Kirschmann, John D, Director with Gayla Kirschmann. _Nutrition Almanac, 4th ed._ New York. McGraw-Hill Book Company, 1996

Kitchen Metrics. Ottawa. Reproduced by Metric Commission Canada with permission from Agriculture Canada

Netzer, Corinne T. _The Complete Book of Food Counts._ New York. Bantam Doubleday Division Publishing Group, Incorporated, 1988

FOR A WELCOME GIFT
GIVE
'HEALTHIER MUFFINS'

Please send _____ copies of Healthier Muffins
at $12.95 plus $3.00 shipping and handling cost per book to:

Name _____

Street _____

City _____ Province _____

Postal Code or Zip _____

Please allow 4 - 6 weeks for delivery.

Make cheque or money order payable to:
E.C. Publishing
2391 Highland Road
Victoria, B.C.
V9E 1K7

Or email ercox@bc.sympatico.ca